T0065414

More Grateful:

A 21-Day Writing Journey to Increase Gratitude

SHERYL WALKER

authorHOUSE®

AuthorHouse™
1663 Liberty Drive
Bloomington, IN 47403
www.authorhouse.com
Phone: 833-262-8899

Published by AuthorHouse 09/23/2020

ISBN: 978-1-6655-0127-9 (sc)
ISBN: 978-1-6655-0126-2 (e)

Library of Congress Control Number: 2020918669

Print information available on the last page.

Any people depicted in stock imagery provided by Getty Images are models, and such images are being used for illustrative purposes only. Certain stock imagery © Getty Images.

This book is printed on acid-free paper.

Scripture quotations marked NIV are taken from the Holy Bible, New International Version®. NIV®. Copyright © 1973, 1978, 1984 by International Bible Society. Used by permission of Zondervan. All rights reserved. [Biblica]

To my Family: You are Joy. I am grateful.

Gratitude Prayer

Lord,
Please allow me to remain in a state of gratitude
Grateful for everything that comes my way
God, I give thanks in all circumstances
The good and the bad
For even through challenges,
There is love
There are blessings
There is abundance
Thank you, God

INTRODUCTION

Having a positive, grateful attitude toward life makes all the difference. When we trust God, we give thanks for everything—yes, even the pain. An attitude of gratitude gives us the patience to endure and wait until the end, knowing God has the final say in everything. It will all work for our good.

Where there is gratitude, we attract even more blessings. Seeing the gift in everything makes life more meaningful and enjoyable. Thank you, God, for the rainbows in the midst of the storm.

As I wrote this book, I reflected on my own life experiences, particularly my blessings and challenges. As I considered the challenges I faced, I came to see that there were always blessings in the midst. Daily writing often serves as an enlightenment ritual for me personally and lifts me out of life's most challenging moments.

This book was written during the COVID-19 pandemic. In the midst of people dying at alarming rates, I gave birth to my second child. I had a less than ideal hospital experience and I was horrified. But at the same time, I knew I was extremely blessed to be able to have a baby during this time. How could I be so blessed in several areas of my life yet be so disappointed with the event that had just taken place? I had to do something with the negative emotions. I was off balance. I must have been focused on the wrong thing. How could I be in the presence of a living miracle, and still be so dissatisfied? I had already learned that my healing was up to me, so I got to work reflecting on this notion of gratitude.

Instead of dwelling on the sorrows of my birthing experience, I decided to switch gears. No person or situation would have so much power over my wellbeing. This led me to reflect on how I could use this season of death, darkness, and uncertainty to give thanks for this miracle I had just birthed, and see the blessings in the trial despite it all. This text focuses on increasing gratitude through consistent daily reflection and writing. Going through each day, one by one, forced me to look at all my circumstances—both good and bad—as blessings. It forced me to seek out the simple blessings throughout the day. It shifted my perspective. Every good thing comes from God. He is in the midst of it all.

Even in silence, God is here. As we endured the COVID-19 pandemic coupled with the senseless killings of black people in America, followed by protests and looting, it felt as if it was a global awakening. What was God saying to us? There was rampant evil, disconnection from our families, each other, and God. We were so blessed, yet we were not operating as such. Nevertheless, we can still express gratitude for the lessons in the storm. We know God is here. He is always here.

In the subsequent pages, you will be presented with daily gratitude passages. This is a series of 21 reflections on gratitude, giving you meditations to carry out day by day. You will also be asked to write each day. Pour your heart out onto the pages that have been provided. Read, reflect, write, and give thanks. I hope that you will benefit from this 21-day journey and by the end be more grateful for all of your blessings.

GRATITUDE ASSIGNMENT 1

Your major assignment for the next 10 days is to fill out your Gratitude T-chart: On the left, track all the good things you take notice of. On the right, track how the enemy attempted to discourage you but it worked out for your good.

Gratitude T-Chart

BLESSINGS	ATTEMPTS AT DISCOURAGEMENT

Now to him who is able to do **immeasurably more than all we ask or imagine**, according to his power that is at work within us.

— Ephesians 3:20 (NIV)

DAY 1

Thank you, God, for all my blessings

Everything is a gift from God. When you sit back and think of all the blessings and abundance God has brought into your life, you can't help but sing hallelujah praises. God is the source of all our blessings.

Health, strength, loved ones, gifts, talents, opportunities, just waking up this morning is a blessing. The list is truly endless.

How God removes us from situations that no longer serve us...

How God promotes and provides for us when the door of opportunity seems closed...

This isn't to say life doesn't have its fair share of challenges. All blessings come with burdens, but even with that in mind, we are truly blessed. Shift your perspective. Remember, every good thing comes from God.

There are three things to focus on today:

1. **Focus on what you do have, and not your lack.** No matter what we get, it seems like we are always longing for more. Also, try not to compare your blessings with someone else's. This is your life, no one else's. If there is something you feel you lack, boldly make your petition to God. Ask and it is given. You have not because you ask not.

2. **Give thanks in all circumstances!** If you reflect on your circumstances, just when you think you have it bad, take some

time to reflect and you will see that God has made a way for you during all of the challenges in your life.

3. **Thank God for your blessings through prayer and praise.** Thank God jubilantly for all he has done. Play hymns of worship. There is a famous line, "What if tomorrow you only got to keep what you were grateful for today? What would you be able to keep?" Be generous with your gratitude to God.

Day 1 Prompt: Reflect on your blessings. What are you grateful for? What has God provided? Write 10 "big" blessings you are grateful for. This could be circumstances and/or individuals in your life. Pick one of the big blessings and write three details about one specific thing or person you are grateful for. Really appreciate all God has done.

_____

_____

_____

_____

_____

_____

_____

_____

_____

_____

_____

_____

_____

_____

_____

_____

_____

_____

_____

_____

Remember to fill in your Gratitude T Chart

Give thanks in all circumstances; for this is
God's will for you in Christ Jesus.

— 1 Thessalonians 5:18 (NIV)

DAY 2

Thank you, God, for the small things

Take notice of:

The sunrise...
Finding a parking spot...
Small acts of kindness throughout the day...
Someone giving you an encouraging word...
Or a token of appreciation ...
Drinking a comforting cup of tea...
Or maybe it's a stranger's sweet smile or hospitable service...
A safe landing...
The affection from a pet...
Long walks in the neighborhood...
A baby's sweet giggle...
A restorative nap...
Food on the table...
Shelter...
Bills paid...
Your health...

The small things are in fact the big things. I used to enjoy making my son's lunch for school every day. I figured if I could get up and do that every day, all was well. God blesses us countless times throughout the day. Are you paying attention? If we get too consumed with life, we will miss it all.

Day 2 Prompt: What are some small or simple blessings you noticed today? Write 3 "small" things you are grateful for.

_____

_____

_____

_____

_____

_____

_____

_____

_____

_____

_____

_____

_____

_____

_____

_____

_____

_____

Remember to fill in your Gratitude T Chart

Always giving thanks to God the Father for everything, in the name of our Lord Jesus Christ.

— Ephesians 5:20 (NIV)

DAY 3

Thank you, God, for allowing me to reframe the unfavorable

In the midst of unfavorable times, it's hard to imagine ALL is for good. Sometimes you have to literally reframe your life and look at things from the perspective of what certain events have taught you and how they have built you up. Write a new story, a new narrative, a different inner dialogue. There was a purpose to everything that has happened in your life. It has shaped who you are today. God gave you the strength to endure, and will continue to supply you with strength.

Consider the job or opportunity that rejected you. In the moment it felt disappointing, but in the long run, it most likely led you to a job that was more suitable for you. These disappointments are opportunities for God to show you he has much more in store. Thank you, God, for blocking what was not meant for me. Thank you for protection.

Consider varying offenses that come your way on a given day. Despite the sting and disappointment of the offense, remain calm and allow God to move. Praise Him anyway. Remain positive. Don't allow negative things to take over your thoughts. God supplies the resilience to withstand any physical, verbal, or emotional attack that comes our way.

There is no way to minimize the tremendous loss some have experienced. Hardships and challenges do however provide opportunities. You learn some of your best life lessons, and those experiences most often become a stepping stone for something else. No pain is wasted. Every crisis has hidden blessings. Struggles indeed make us stronger, and may carve a new path that might have otherwise not been revealed. Thank you, God, for the inner peace in knowing all the events and circumstances in my life come together for my good. The pain might inspire a poem, song, or book that serves to encourage others. It might allow me to be a source of comfort and support when a family or friend endures a similar battle.

<u>Day 3 Prompt</u>: Reframe an unfavorable situation. How did that situation prove to have a purpose? Can you see how the "worst of times" were the "best of times"? Write three details about one specific challenging situation you are now grateful for. What were some of the blessings in the trial?

_____

_____

_____

_____

_____

_____

_____

_____

_____

_____

_____

_____

_____

_____

_____

_____

_____

_____

Remember to fill in your Gratitude T Chart

He is the one you praise; **he is your God, who performed for you those great and awesome wonders** you saw with your own eyes.

— Deuteronomy 10:21 (NIV)

DAY 4

Thank you, God, for miracles

What was a true miracle that has happened lately? Have you ever been in need of a supernatural provision and it shows up unexpectedly? I consider being sick and God sending the right person with the right remedy to heal me. Or thinking a situation was impossible and God surprises me with help in an unexpected form, making a way out of no way.

In the Bible, Jesus took two fish and five loaves of bread and fed 5,000 people. Imagine: we were in the midst of a pandemic, and despite its devastations, some people were fully healed. Babies were still being born. There were supernatural blessings in the midst of the trial. God's miracles, despite challenges, are a reminder of who He is and how much He loves us. If He could craft such an amazing design just for me, everything in my life must serve a purpose—the good and the bad.

I recall questioning God about why he had me in a particular situation, that had presented so many incredible challenges. Slowly but surely, in time, God showed me why this was my assignment. Despite the challenge of the situation, there were many moments it felt like God sent a team of angels just to protect me! Sometimes God uses us as the miracle for someone else and a miracle circle emerges. We can be a miracle for someone, and that person then becomes a miracle for someone or something else. God, please use me as a miracle in someone else's life where you see fit.

Day 4 Prompt: Reflect on a recent miracle. What has God provided on a supernatural level? Write three details about one specific miracle you are grateful for.

_____

_____

_____

_____

_____

_____

_____

_____

_____

_____

_____

_____

_____

_____

_____

_____

_____

_____

_____

_____

Remember to fill in your Gratitude T Chart

The Lord is good to those whose hope is in him,
to the one who seeks him;
**it is good to wait quietly
for the salvation of the Lord**.

— Lamentations 3:25-26 (NIV)

DAY 5

Thank you, God, for your perfect timing

There is a divine order to life events and nothing good happens accidentally. I recall begging God for a baby. My child did not arrive when I wanted him to, but in retrospect, I thank God my baby arrived when he did. A blessing given too soon is not a blessing at all. For example, God might allow a bad relationship to persist for long enough so when the good relationship comes along, you really appreciate it. There is wisdom in his timing. He might allow you to grow and develop at a particular job so that when there is a new opportunity for promotion, you will have experienced all that is needed for that new assignment.

God's timing of events is very clever. He comes through for us in ways we would never imagine.

Day 5 Prompt: Reflect on God's timing. What is something God delayed, expedited, or rearranged for your benefit? Write three details about one specific divinely timed circumstance you are grateful for.

_____

_____

_____

_____

_____

_____

_____

_____

_____

_____

_____

_____

_____

_____

_____

_____

_____

_____

Remember to fill in your Gratitude T Chart

He will **command his angels concerning you**
to guard you carefully;

— Luke 4:10 (NIV)

DAY 6

Thank you, God, for the angels you place in our lives

Consider people that show up—family, friends, and strangers alike—during times of need or as sources of relief. I recall being at work with no clue how to perform a task that had a time constraint. It had to be completed that day. A coworker sacrificed her day to show me how to complete the task. I needed the right help, and God sent the perfect person to help me.

I also recall times being sick and God sending the right caretakers to care for me. God places these angels in our lives to be loyal to us and show up for us in a time of need. They serve as true angels on earth. We can't do life alone. God sends special people to us, for us to love, and for us to be loved by.

Day 6 Prompt: Think about an everyday angel you have encountered in your life. Have you been fortunate to have key people serve as angels in your time of need, as a source of relief, or a breath of fresh air? Write 5 details about one specific "angel" you are grateful for, who showed up unexpectedly.

_____

_____

_____

_____

_____

_____

_____

_____

_____

_____

_____

_____

_____

_____

_____

_____

_____

_____

_____

_____

_____

Remember to fill in your Gratitude T Chart

I will extol the Lord at all times;
his praise will always be on my lips.
I will glory in the Lord;
let the afflicted hear and rejoice.
Glorify the Lord with me;
let us exalt his name together.

— Psalm 34:1-3 (NIV)

DAY 7

Thank you, God, that life is working for me, and not against me

Consider all the things that are currently going right in your life, and which seem to align with what you were meant to do and who you are meant to be. Despite the gap between where you are and where you want to be, some things are just pretty good. How is the universe conspiring on your behalf right now? Thoughts become things. Thoughts come back as experiences. Are you focused on life's current favorable circumstances?

Day 7 Prompt: Reflect on what is currently going well right now. Take one minute to visualize this in your mind. Write three details about one specific thing that is "going right" at this point in time.

_____

_____

_____

_____

_____

_____

_____

_____

_____

_____

_____

_____

_____

_____

_____

_____

_____

_____

_____

Remember to fill in your Gratitude T Chart

I will praise you, Lord, with all my heart;
before the "gods" I will sing your praise.
I will bow down toward your holy temple
and will praise your name
for your unfailing love and your faithfulness,
for you have so exalted your solemn decree
that it surpasses your fame.

— Psalm 138:1-2 (NIV)

DAY 8

Thank you, God, for places and spaces that feel like home

Where feels like home to you? For me it's anywhere with learning. It is a place and space where my gifts and work are aligned. I always feel at home at a school. I know that education and caring for the educational growth of others is aligned to my life's purpose. Perhaps home for you could be places and spaces where you are helping. It could be places and spaces where you are using a talent. It is a place that allows you to operate in your calling. I thank God for showing me where "home" is. It naturally fills us up.

Day 8 Prompt: Where is home for you? When and where do you feel like your true self? It's a place and space that fills up your love tank. It is a space of fulfillment. Write three reasons why you are grateful for your "home." If you don't know "home," ask God to reveal it to you.

_____

_____

_____

_____

_____

_____

_____

_____

_____

_____

_____

_____

_____

_____

_____

_____

_____

_____

_____

_____

Remember to fill in your Gratitude T Chart

Give praise to the Lord, proclaim his name;
make known among the nations what he has done.
Sing to him, sing praise to him;
tell of all his wonderful acts.
Glory in his holy name;
let the hearts of those who seek the Lord rejoice.

— Psalm 105:1-3 (NIV)

DAY 9

Thank you, God, for breath and good health

It is such a beautiful gift to be alive and in good health. It is often when those around us are perishing that we really value our own lives even more. Don't take life for granted. Each waking day is a chance to celebrate and glorify God. It is also an opportunity to be a blessing to others. Life is truly a gift, despite its many challenges.

I remember a man once telling me, "Physically healthy people have no right to be unhappy." Consider those that did not wake up this morning, leaving family members to mourn deeply. Consider those that are suffering due to poor health, who are bound by pain, or unable to move around and live freely. There are many people that have to rely on others for their basic mobility. If you have the gift of breath and good health, you have much to be grateful for.

Day 9 Prompt: Take a deep breath. Write three reasons why having breath and good health is something you are grateful for.

_____

_____

_____

_____

_____

_____

_____

_____

_____

_____

_____

_____

_____

_____

_____

_____

_____

Remember to fill in your Gratitude T Chart

And do not forget to **do good and to share with others**, for with such sacrifices God is pleased.

— Hebrews 13:16 (NIV)

DAY 10

Thank you, God, for opportunities to affirm, bless, and serve others with good

Whatever gifts you have, you must give them away and serve others. We are all born with an immense amount of capabilities and talents. These gifts are to be used. Give them away freely to others. This is your sacrifice. If you can connect with the youth, become a youth volunteer. If you have a gift of listening, be a listening ear to those that need to talk. Cease looking at things from the perspective of what you can get out of the situation, and consider what you can give to the situation by serving others with your talents, resources, and time.

Day 10 Prompt: Reflect on your gifts and talents. Write out three opportunities you have had in the past to serve others with your gifts. Expand on your gratitude for those opportunities.

_____

_____

_____

_____

_____

_____

_____

_____

_____

_____

_____

_____

_____

_____

_____

_____

_____

_____

_____

_____

Remember to fill in your Gratitude T Chart

GRATITUDE ASSIGNMENT 2

Your next major assignment is to write one "Perspective-Shifting Statement" every day for the next ten days. These statements shift what is perceived as a negative situation into gratitude.

Examples of "Perspective-Shifting Statements":

My child is frustrating me.
Well, you have a child;
Many wish they could have a child.

My supervisor is stressing me out.
Well, you are blessed to have a job.

My parents …
But they are alive.

This person is upsetting me.
Well, when I consider the kindness they showed me when they…
Or that they taught me…
Or provided me with…
I feel gratitude in my heart and release the animosity I feel right now.
What they have given me is more than enough.

Perspective-Shifting Statements:

Use this space to write 5 perspective-shifting statements. Shift 5 negative situations into statements of gratitude.

1. _____

2. _____

3. _____

4. _____

5. _____

Jabez cried out to the God of Israel, "Oh, that you would **bless me and enlarge my territory**! Let your hand be with me, and **keep me from harm** so that I will be free from pain." And God granted his request.

— 1 Chronicles 4:10 (NIV)

DAY 11

Thank you, God, for places and spaces that can handle my enormity

Not everywhere is able to handle your greatness. The good thing is that any place or space God has for you to be, you shall dwell there. No man can change God's divine plan for your life. If you are there, then God decreed that for your life. My prayer is that if a place cannot handle all I have to offer, Lord please expand my territory. Place me where my gifts are needed, appreciated, and can be used for your glory. Thank you, God, for planning out our lives in such detail that you will always have a seat waiting for us at the table. If I am here, it was your plan for me to be here. Thank You, God, that my steps are ordered.

Day 11 Prompt: Consider a place or space that was able to handle your greatness. The red carpet was rolled out, they utilized your gifts, and appreciated your service. Write three reasons why you are grateful for that opportunity.

_____

_____

_____

_____

_____

_____

_____

_____

_____

_____

_____

_____

_____

_____

_____

_____

_____

_____

_____

_____

Remember to write one perspective shifting statement

Wait for the Lord;
be strong and take heart
and wait for the Lord.

— Psalm 27:14 (NIV)

DAY 12

Thank you, God, for patience so that I can cease complaining and wait well

God's timing is supreme and well worth the wait. It is through waiting that he perfects our character. We tend to worship and exalt our problems, but instead we should worship and exalt God. Nothing lasts forever, and there will be an end to our suffering.

Wait well, with expectancy and faith. Enjoy your life as you wait for God to move. Rid yourself of dissatisfaction, comparison, and complaint. The Israelites complained, and that kept them in captivity for even longer. Complaining is a distraction and the opposite of gratitude. It kills creativity. When we endure, fighting only when directed to do so, the breakthrough seems to come much faster.

Being in a challenging situation has benefits. Knowing what you don't want is just as important as knowing what you do want. A situation you dislike might be a message to pivot your attention and head down a different path. Waiting strengthens your faith in God.

Day 12 Prompt: Reflect on the waiting season. Write out three opportunities you have had during the "wait." What have been blessings during the waiting? What have you learned? How has your character been perfected?

_____

_____

_____

_____

_____

_____

_____

_____

_____

_____

_____

_____

_____

_____

_____

_____

_____

_____

_____

_____

Remember to write one perspective shifting statement

Do everything in love.

— 1 Corinthians 16:14 (NIV)

DAY 13

Thank you, God, for expressions of love and care

To love and be loved is life's greatest treasure. It is truly a demonstration of God and the best of all the human experiences. It fills the soul.

It feels wonderful when someone genuinely shows that they care about you. When someone goes out of their way to show an expression of love, we should never take it for granted. This could be as simple as

- Saying kind or encouraging words
- Truly listening and acting on what someone is saying
- Reaching out when someone crosses your mind to check in on them
- Smiling
- Showing affection with a hug
- Giving up your time
- Being there for someone when they need you
- Sending someone flowers or another small token
- Accepting them fully for who they are, weaknesses and all
- Being mindful of the words you use
- Celebrating a person
- Praying together and for that person
- Sacrificing

- Being honest with someone
- Apology and changed behavior

Be generous with your expressions of gratitude toward others. Thank you, God, for anyone who has ever expressed genuine care toward me.

Day 13 Prompt: Write down three expressions of love and care that have been shown toward you in the past few weeks. Expand on how they made you feel and why you are so grateful.

_____

_____

_____

_____

_____

_____

_____

_____

_____

_____

_____

_____

_____

_____

_____

_____

_____

_____

_____

_____

_____

Remember to write one perspective shifting statement

May the God of hope **fill you with all joy and peace** as you trust in him, so that you may **overflow with hope** by the power of the Holy Spirit.

— Romans 15:13 (NIV)

DAY 14

Thank you, God, for reasons to smile and be happy

There are so many reasons to be happy and to smile, despite external conditions. Try your best to shift your focus when you find yourself in a state of sadness. The secret to happiness is to do more of the things that bring you happiness. The best thing we can do for this world is to monitor our own levels of happiness. When do you get a happy boost?

My happiness increases when I

- Talk to children
- Engage in a good conversation with a friend or loved one
- Relax in a book store
- Watch a good documentary
- Laugh
- Pray
- Enjoy what I have instead of excessively yearning for what I don't have
- Learn something new
- Create positive moments with friends, my spouse, children, parents, siblings, nieces and nephews, and other extended family
- Sing a song I love out loud
- Eat delicious food at a beautiful restaurant
- Take time to truly rest

Day 14 Prompt: What makes you happy? Whatever it is, do more of it. Life is such a short and precious gift. Reflect on three things you are grateful for because they evoke feelings of happiness.

_____

_____

_____

_____

_____

_____

_____

_____

_____

_____

_____

_____

_____

_____

_____

_____

_____

_____

Remember to write one perspective shifting statement

A new command I give you: **Love one another**. As I
have loved you, so you must love one another.

— John 13:34 (NIV)

DAY 15

Thank you, God, for sacred moments of joy with loved ones

Play outside with your child, visit a family member, attend the school gathering, the bridal shower, the wedding, and the party, and fully enjoy it. These are sacred moments, set up with the intention of joy. Do not simply attend, but bring your most positive, well-intentioned self to that gathering. These are the positive happy memories that will string together all the "good times" our life is comprised of.

All we have is now. We can plan to attend the next party, but how do we know there is a next party, or that we will even make it to see the next party? Treat sacred moments with loved ones with reverence. The greatest gift we can give others is our time. Cherish these moments. Bring your whole heart to the festivity. Leave all criticism and negativity behind. Thank them openly for their time, the joy, and positive memories they created with you.

Day 15 Prompt: Reflect on three recent joyous moments with family and friends. Why are you grateful for those moments? In what ways were these moments "sacred"?

_____

_____

_____

_____

_____

_____

_____

_____

_____

_____

_____

_____

_____

_____

_____

_____

_____

_____

_____

_____

_____

Remember to write one perspective shifting statement

God is our **refuge and strength**,
an ever-present **help in trouble**.
Therefore we will not fear, though the earth give way
and the mountains fall into the heart of the sea,
though its waters roar and foam
and the mountains quake with their surging.
There is a river whose streams make glad the city of God,
the holy place where the Most High dwells.
God is within her, she will not fall;
God will help her at break of day.
Nations are in uproar, kingdoms fall;
he lifts his voice, the earth melts.
The Lord Almighty is with us;
the God of Jacob is our fortress.

— Psalm 46:1-7 (NIV)

DAY 16

Thank you, God, for your companionship out of the darkness and into the light

While in a dark place, it's hard to imagine moving into the light. It feels as if life as you know it has been altered. Remember: God is always with you and waiting to hold your hand through the darkness. He is our refuge in any circumstance. It is really just a bend in the road—a detour, so to speak.

Every scary moment filled with fear and stress is an opportunity to lean on God for protection and supernatural strength. Nothing lasts forever, the good or the bad, but I thank you God for walking alongside me during the darkest moments in life. It is this faith and hope that helps us endure. We can reflect on his promises, his past track record, and his unfathomable love. With God, we have nothing to fear.

Day 16 Prompt: Consider a past dark moment. Write three details about your gratitude to God for moving you through it, and into the light. Thank God for serving as your protector and for allowing the outcome to be much better than you anticipated.

Remember to write one perspective shifting statement

Then you will call on me and come and **pray
to me**, and I will listen to you.

— Jeremiah 29:12

DAY 17

Thank you, God, for the gift of prayer

Call out to God through prayer. Prayer is the most powerful tool you have. Prayer provides us with a direct line to God. A line that creates a connection that is everlasting! Prayer shifts things. Thank you, God, for this gift you have given us to communicate and draw closer to you. This allows us to know you. It is a steadfast tool that can be used during the good and bad times. Knowing you allows me to feel covered, protected, and never alone. When we are close to God, we are invincible. Lord, allow me to not only talk to you through prayer, but to pour my heart out to you, so that you can help fight my battles. You consistently supply me with the strength to endure. Allow me to use the gift of prayer to thank you for all you have done, continue to do, and are yet to do in my life.

Day 17 Prompt: Say a prayer to God. Write three details about why you are grateful for your access to God through prayer.

_____

_____

_____

_____

_____

_____

_____

_____

_____

_____

_____

_____

_____

_____

_____

_____

_____

_____

_____

_____

_____

Remember to write one perspective shifting statement

Before I formed you in the womb I knew you,
before you were born **I set you apart**;
I appointed you as a prophet to the nations

— Jeremiah 1:5

DAY 18

Thank you, God, for planting the dream and bringing it to fruition

It is God who gifts us with our talents and supernatural abilities. It is also God who plants the dreams in our hearts and sees them through to their realization. Thank you, God, for answering my prayers even before I ask them, and seeing them become a reality in your perfect timing. We tend to worry if certain things will ever truly come to pass. If we remain faithful and obedient, they often do, and if they don't, God has something even better in store.

Day 18 Prompt: Reflect on a dream that came true. Write three details as to why you are grateful this dream came to pass.

_____
_____
_____
_____
_____
_____
_____
_____
_____
_____
_____
_____
_____
_____
_____
_____
_____
_____

Remember to write one perspective shifting statement

Be devoted to one another in love. Honor
one another above yourselves.

— Romans 12:10

DAY 19

Thank you, God, for authentic connections

It is such a refreshing feeling when you and another person just click. They just get you. You get them. There is mutual acceptance. There is support. They look out for you and you do the same for them. You enjoy the strengths each person brings to the relationship. There is no need for comparison. You balance each other out. You can share in joyous moments filled with smiles and laughter. There is no need to over-explain and justify who you are. You may or may not share similar life experiences, but there is an unspoken bond between you and that person. You can be vulnerable. These connections are refreshing. Thank you, God, for friendships and associations that work well. Their presence is like a breath of fresh air. It warms the soul. If and when you find these connections in a lifetime, cherish them. They are rare and should be treasured.

Day 19 Prompt: Reflect on three authentic connections. Write a detail for each, as to why you are grateful for these connections.

_____

_____

_____

_____

_____

_____

_____

_____

_____

_____

_____

_____

_____

_____

_____

_____

_____

_____

_____

Remember to write one perspective shifting statement

Do not be anxious about anything, but in every situation, by prayer and petition, with thanksgiving, **present your requests to God**. And the peace of God, which transcends all understanding, will guard your hearts and your minds in Christ Jesus.

— Philippians 4:6-7 (NIV)

DAY 20

Thank you, God, for giving me peace

Those that know God have a quiet confidence and peace. We have a testimony. We have had to trust God even when we did not understand why. We have seen God do some amazing things in our life and in the lives of those we love. He did it before and he will do it again.

Peace is beautiful. No excessive wrestling back and forth mentally. The burden of worry is lifted. This Holy confidence allows us to endure, forgive, overcome worry and fear of slights, accept people for who they are and what has shaped their behavior, erect the appropriate boundaries in our lives, and completely surrender. Peace reminds us that competition is futile. There is abundance for us all. There is always enough. Peace is releasing what's not in my control.

While we are human and can swing in and out of bouts of fear and worry, through prayer and petition, we can always return to God's endless reservoir of peace.

Day 20 Prompt: Reflect on three peaceful moments you have had recently. What were the external conditions that contributed to that peace? Why are you grateful?

_____

_____

_____

_____

_____

_____

_____

_____

_____

_____

_____

_____

_____

_____

_____

_____

_____

Remember to write one perspective shifting statement

You will seek me and find me when you seek me with all your heart.

— Jeremiah 29:13 (NIV)

DAY 21

Thank you, God, for making your presence known

Where have you felt God's presence today? He is present at all times. There are these key moments that you know God is there. You might hear His still small voice, or witness one of His miracles. He might give you peace about a situation that could have possibly sent you over the edge.

You recover from illness, or perhaps find out a situation you thought you wanted or needed was an unfavorable situation and God blocked it. You have an emergency with no clue how it will work out, and then it works out perfectly.

Every "oh what a coincidence" is God. Every "can you believe how nicely that worked out" is also God. God truly makes a way out of no way.

Each time you have an epiphany, revelation, or some wisdom is revealed, that too is God. God is our source of learning, growth, and transformation. Every positive change or evolution in our character and disposition—is God. Every spark of creativity and genius is God. Every good and perfect gift is from God!

Day 21 Prompt: Reflect on a blessing that has taken place and you can unequivocally say, "that was God." Write three details as to why this moment was so meaningful to you.

_____

_____

_____

_____

_____

_____

_____

_____

_____

_____

_____

_____

_____

_____

_____

_____

_____

_____

_____

_____

Remember to write one perspective shifting statement

CONCLUSION

Thank you, God, in advance, for what you are about to do.

Thank you, God, for shifting my energy and perspective over the last 21 days.

Thank you, God, for hope.

Thank you, God, for the rainbow in the midst of the clouds.

Your gratitude journey does not end here. Continue to write things you are grateful for each and every day. Regularly write or verbally express statements of gratitude to the many significant people in your life—whether or not you give it to them. Don't forget to use your Gratitude T-chart and Perspective-Shifting Statements daily. Do whatever it takes to shift your energy to focus on all God has done.

Finally, gratitude to you for taking this journey! What you appreciate appreciates. The best is yet to come!

ABOUT THE AUTHOR

Sheryl Walker is an educator and has facilitated 100+ one-on-one adult coaching conversations. Her writing is inspired by her own life journey and those she has coached professionally. Her books are centered around personal growth through the acquisition of new learning, self-reflection, and daily writing. Daily writing has often served as an enlightenment ritual for her personally as a way to endure life's most challenging moments. She is also the author of the books *Waiting Well: A 21-day Writing Journey to Increase Patience, Forgive Anyway: A 30-day Writing Journey to Total Forgiveness*, and *Love Poems to God*. She enjoys writing in her leisure.

Printed in the United States
By Bookmasters